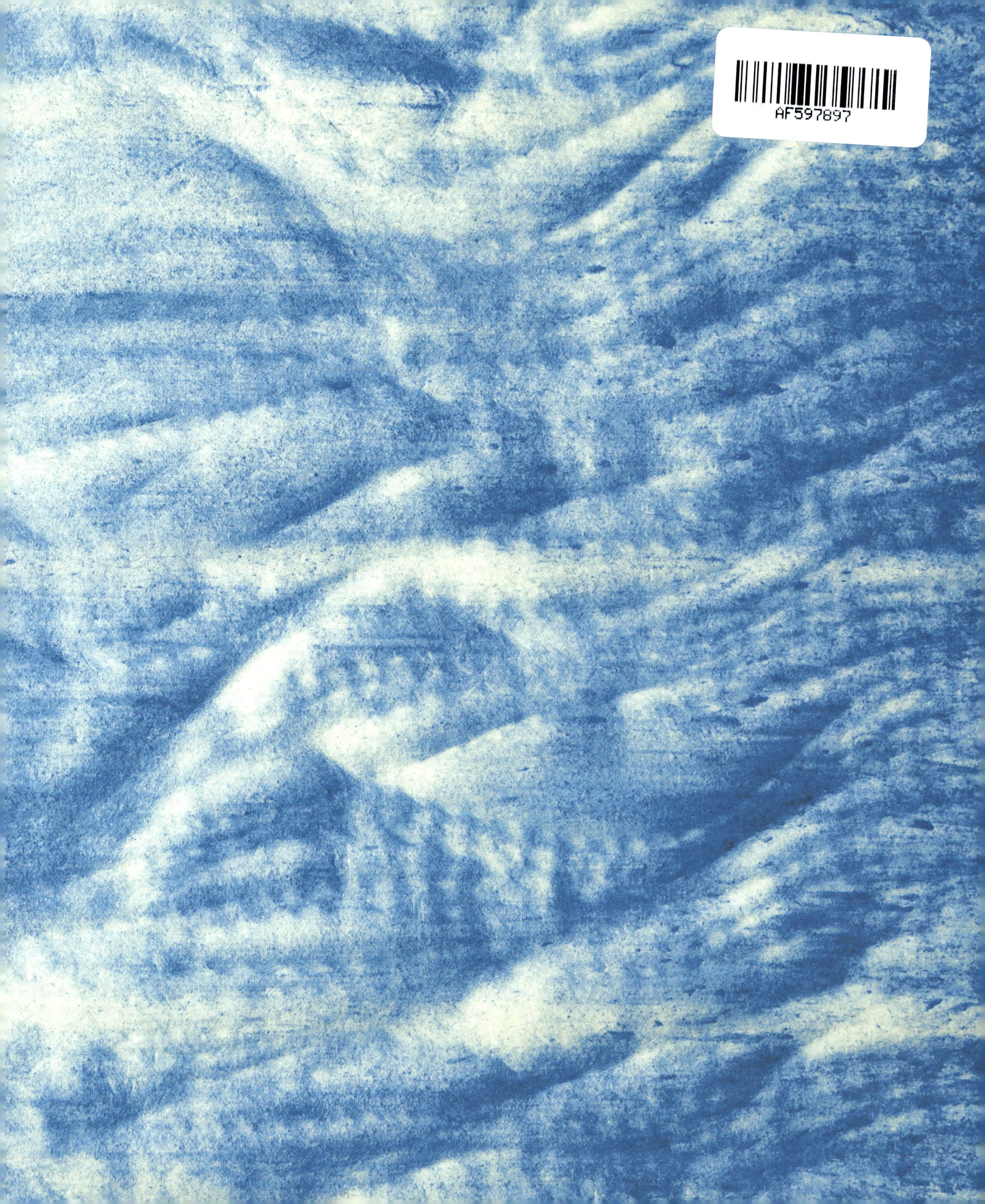

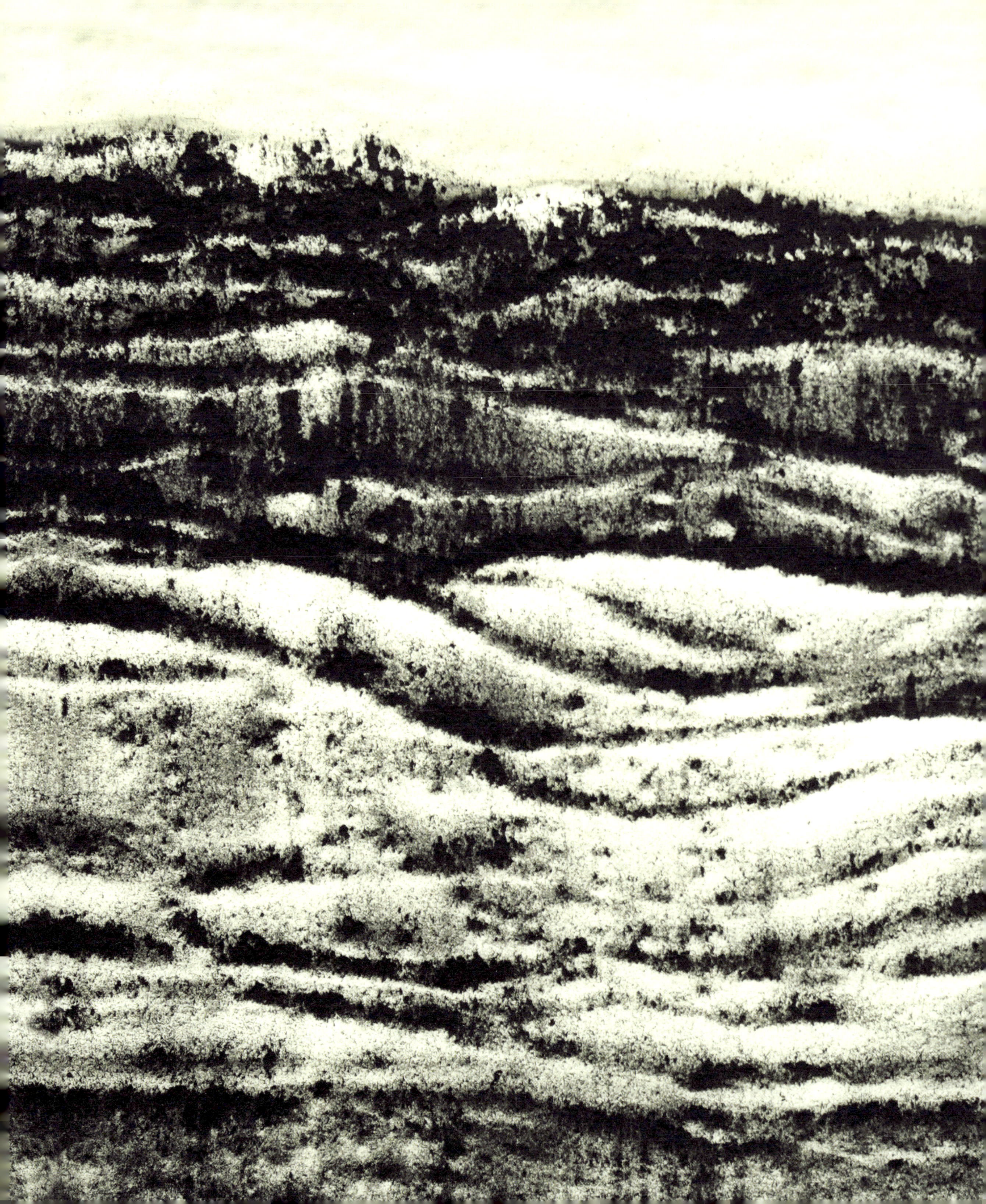

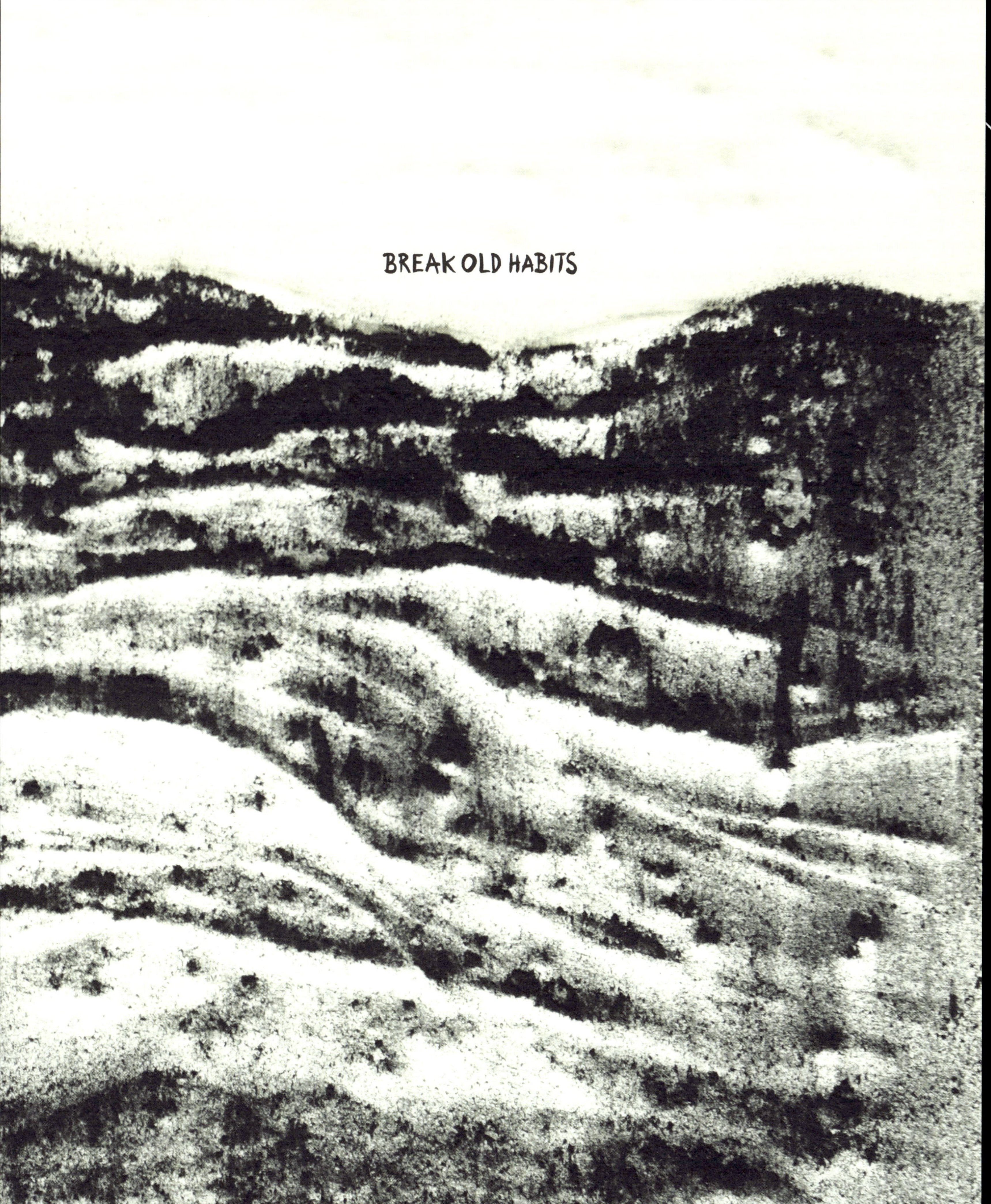
BREAK OLD HABITS

BREAK OLD HABITS

PEPE MOLL DE ALBA

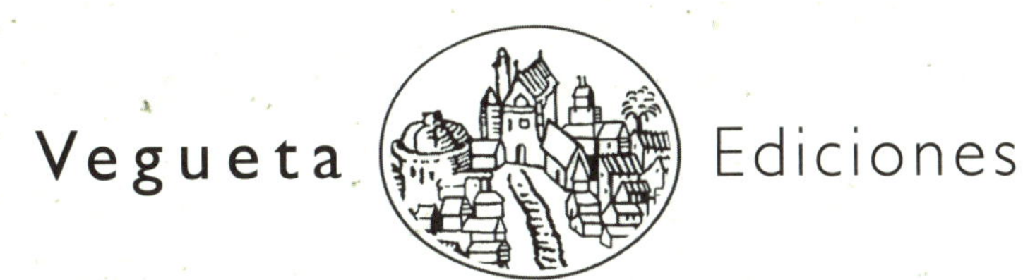

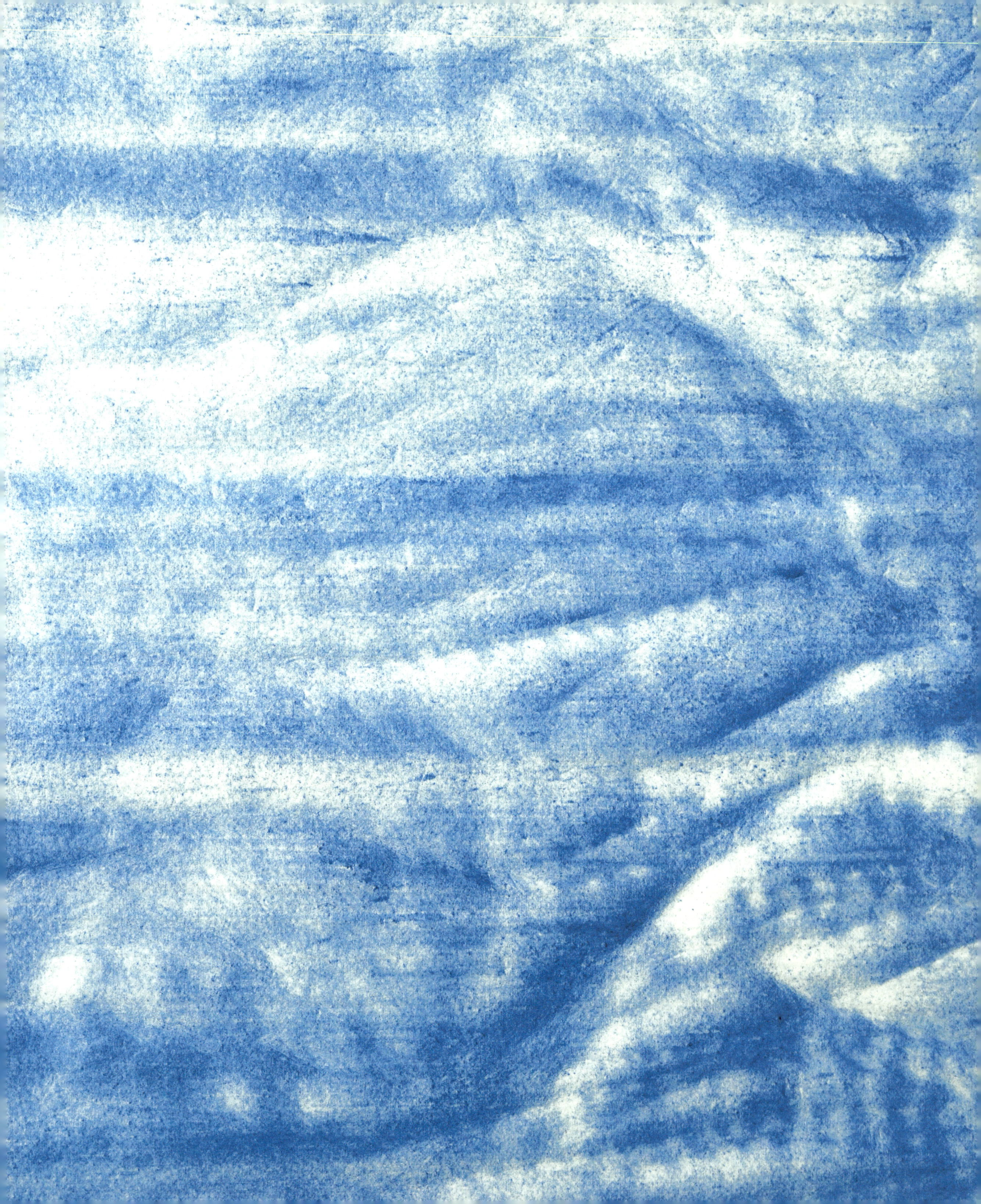

You say this is the end,

that although it seems to move,
it is actually dead,

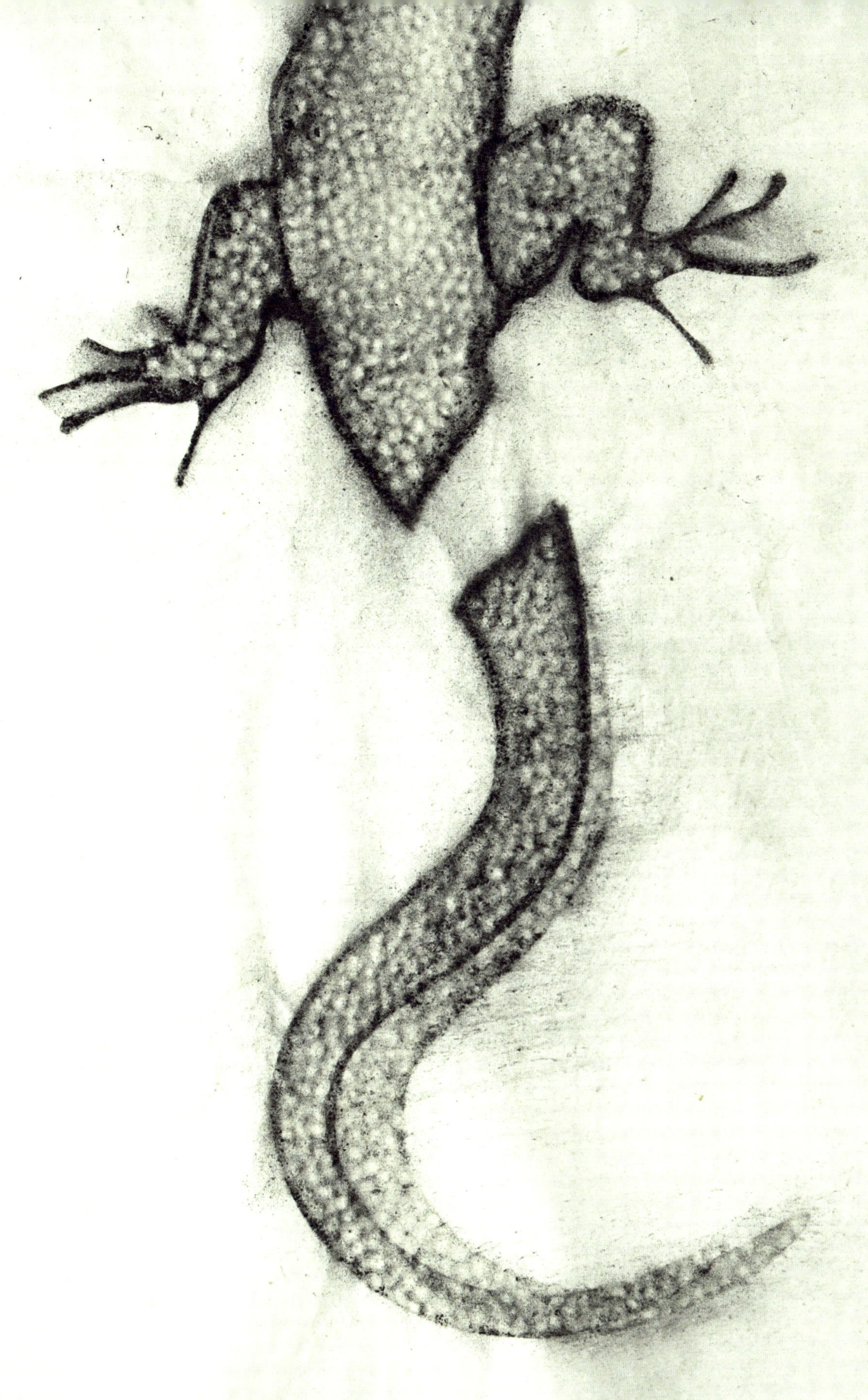

DEAD BUT MOVING

that fantasies
have become unnecessary,

CUT
THE
STRING

that a sudden shift is on its way.

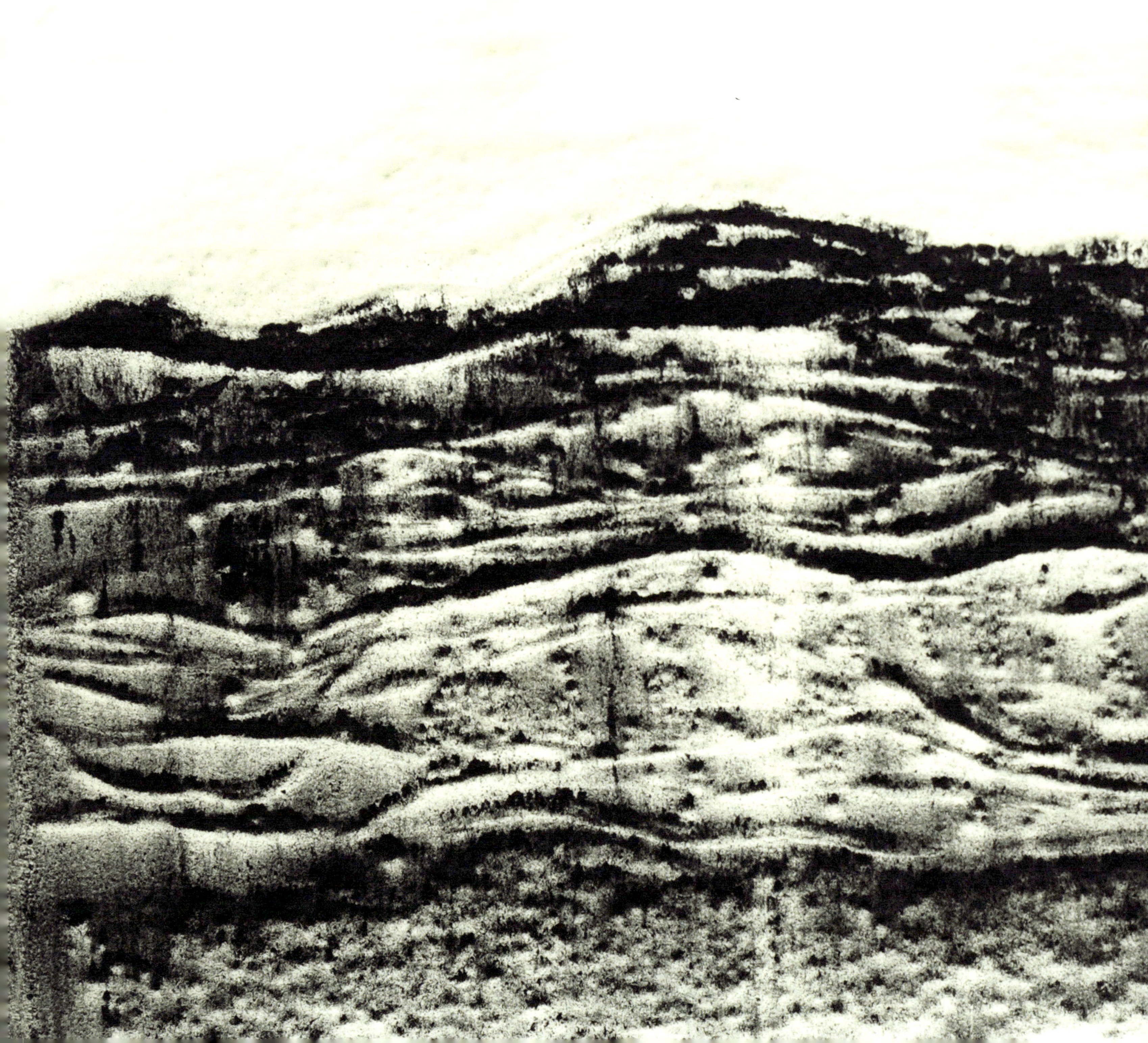

STORM

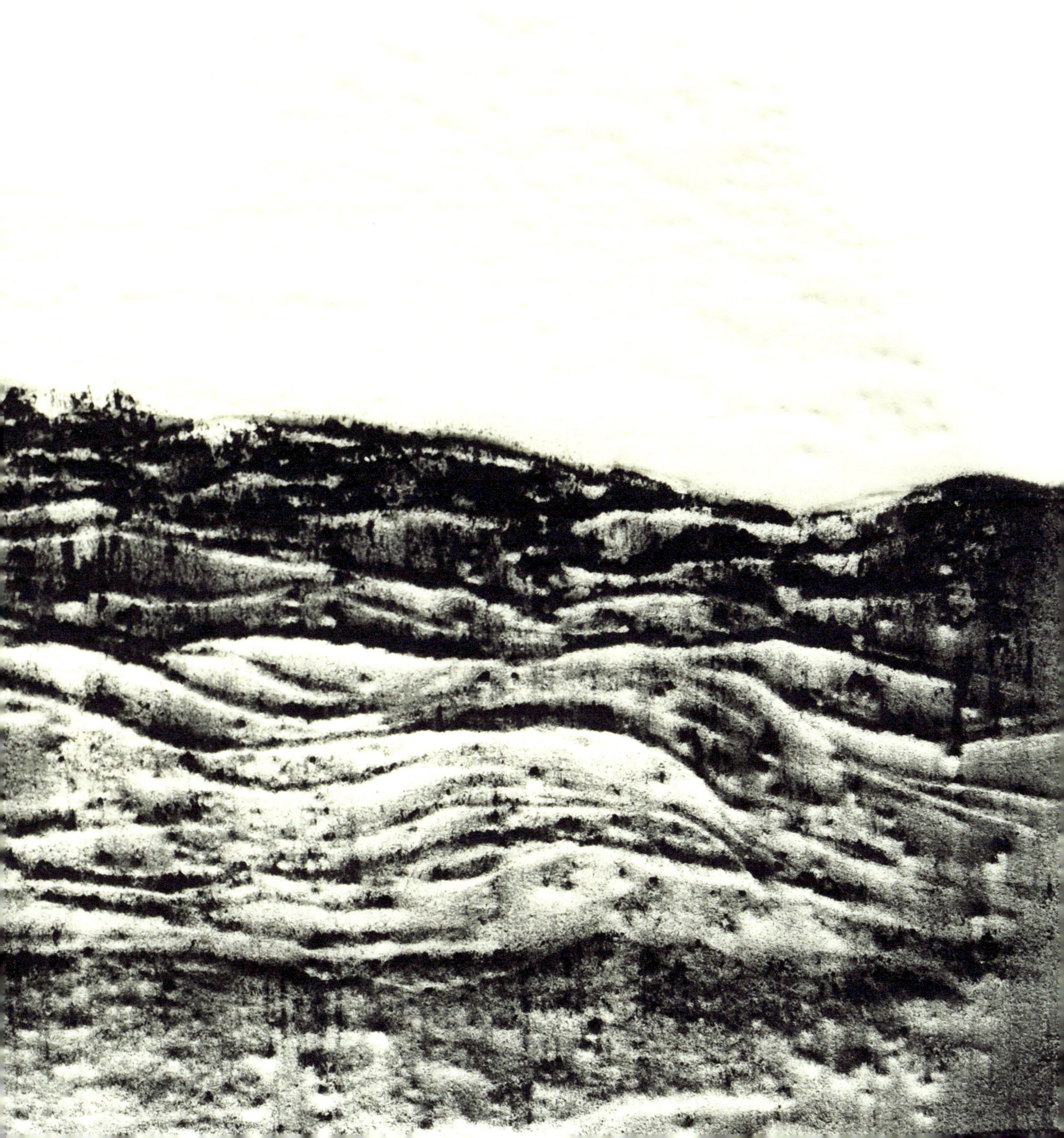

How to remain intact
in the face of the storm?

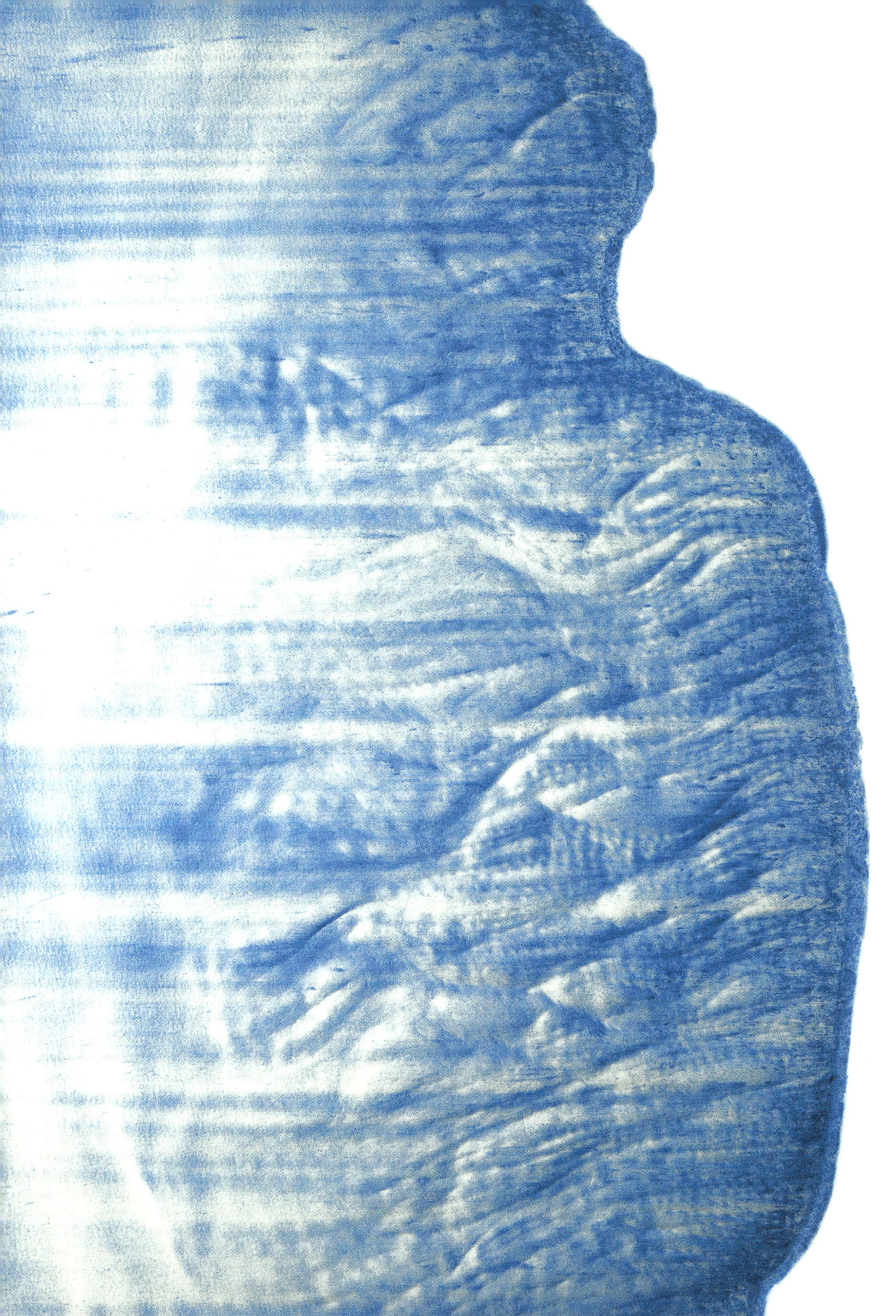

WISDOM

Break old habits
and abandon obsolete mindsets.

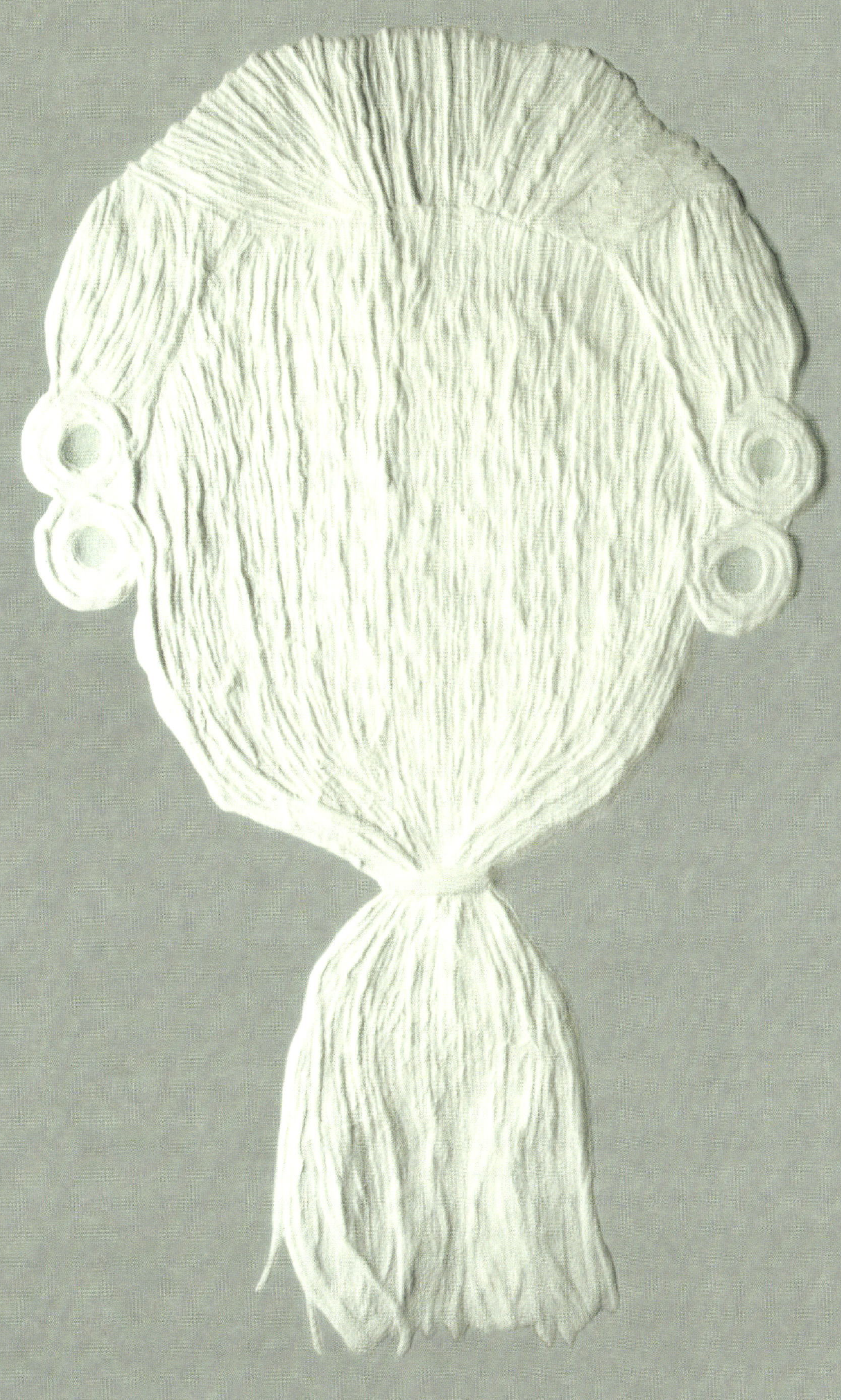

BREAK OLD HABITS

Breathe
and ease your thoughts.

SEE

Clear the mind,
isolate it for a moment.

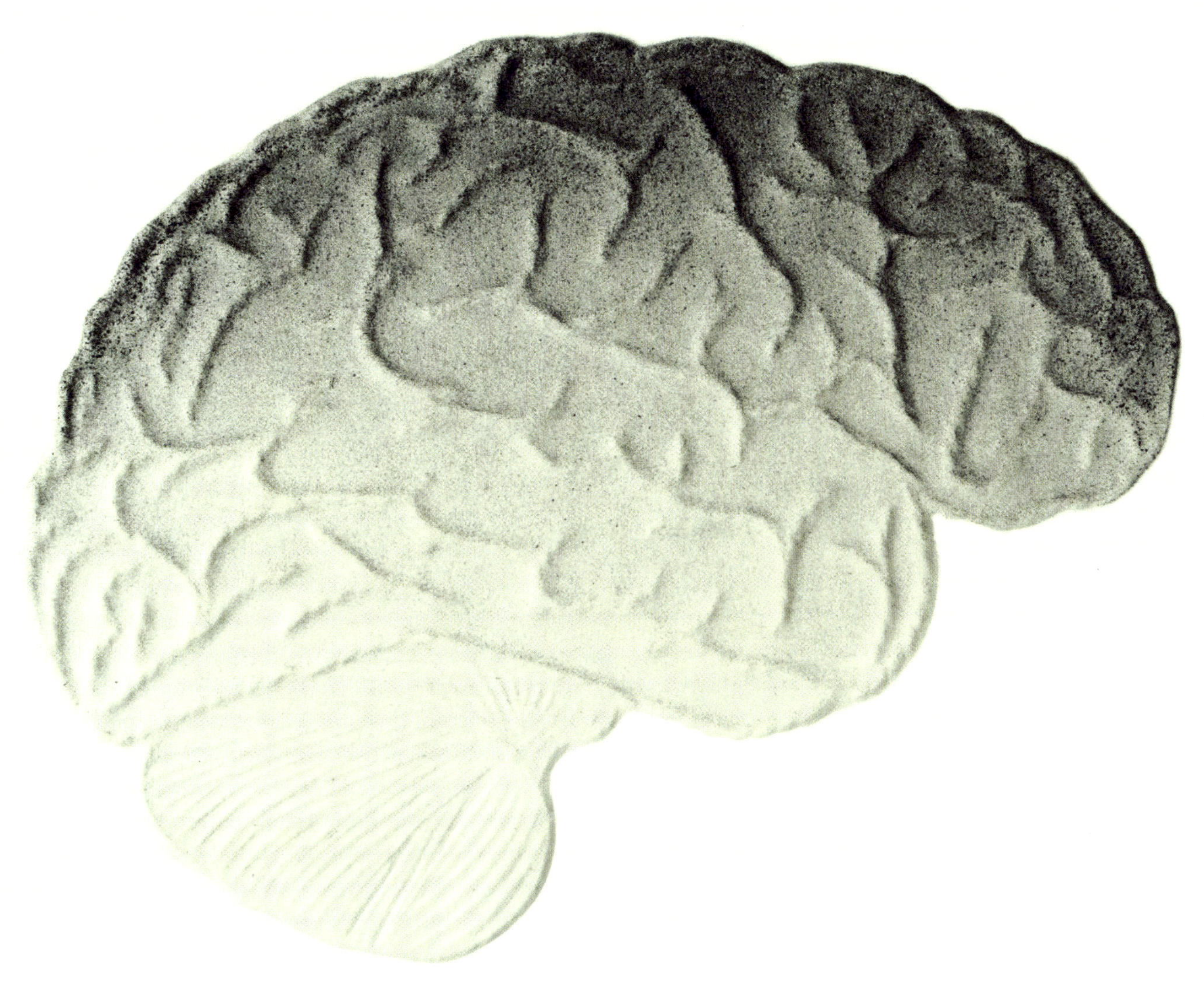

CLEANSE

Feel a perfect emptiness
and find tranquility.

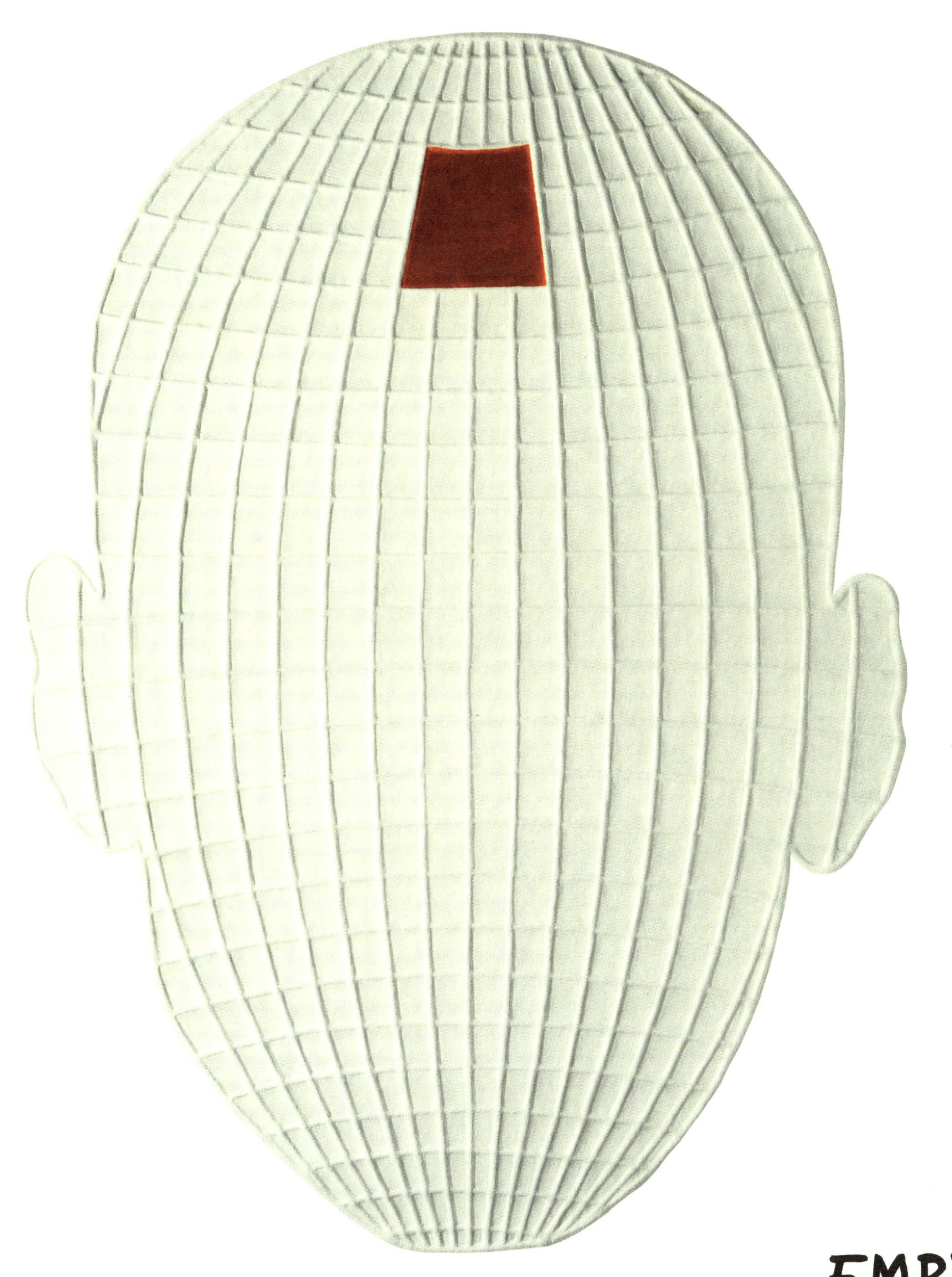

EMPTY

Move the roots
and mingle them with other roots.

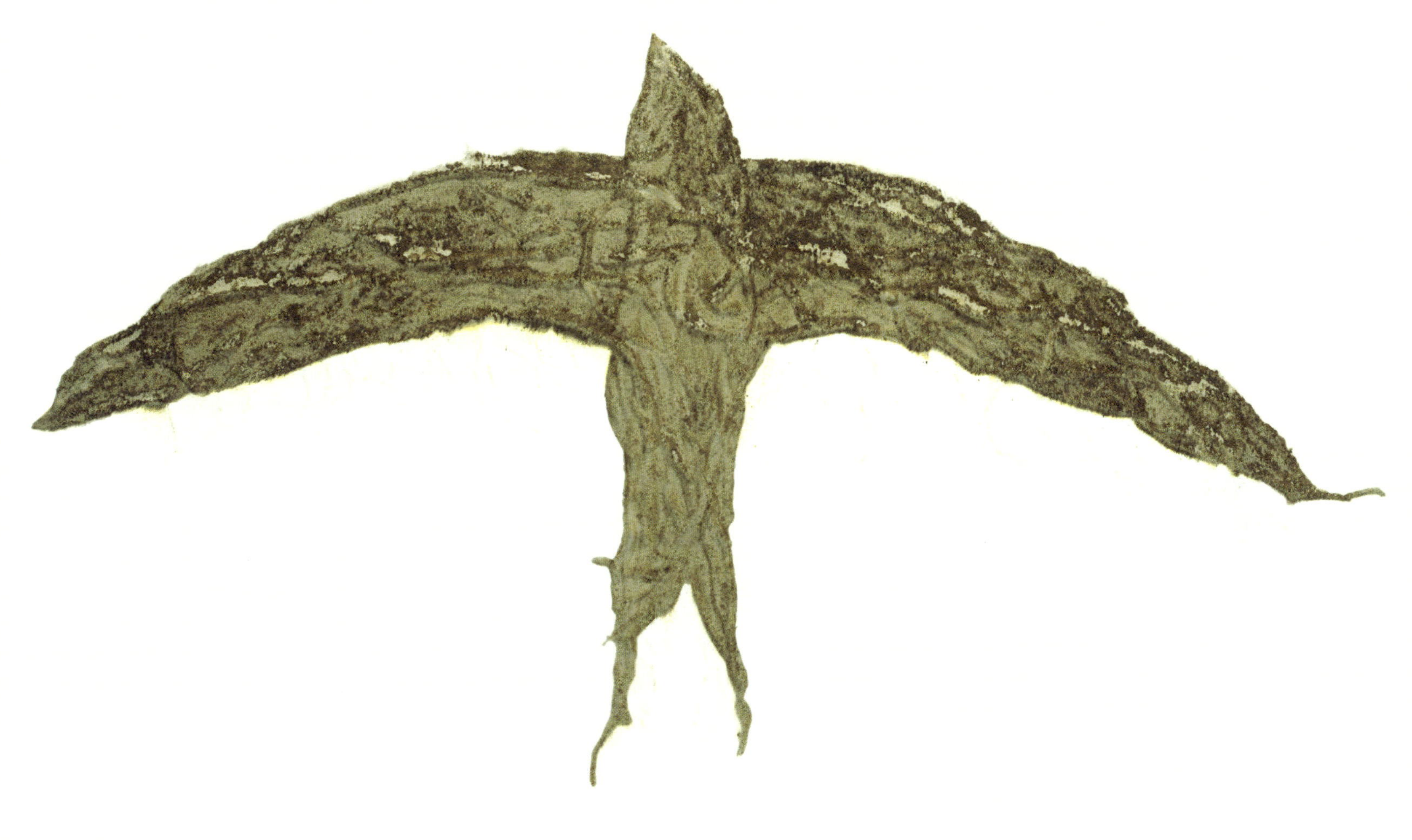

FLYING ROOTS

Love and let yourself be loved,
unafraid of being replaced and forgotten.

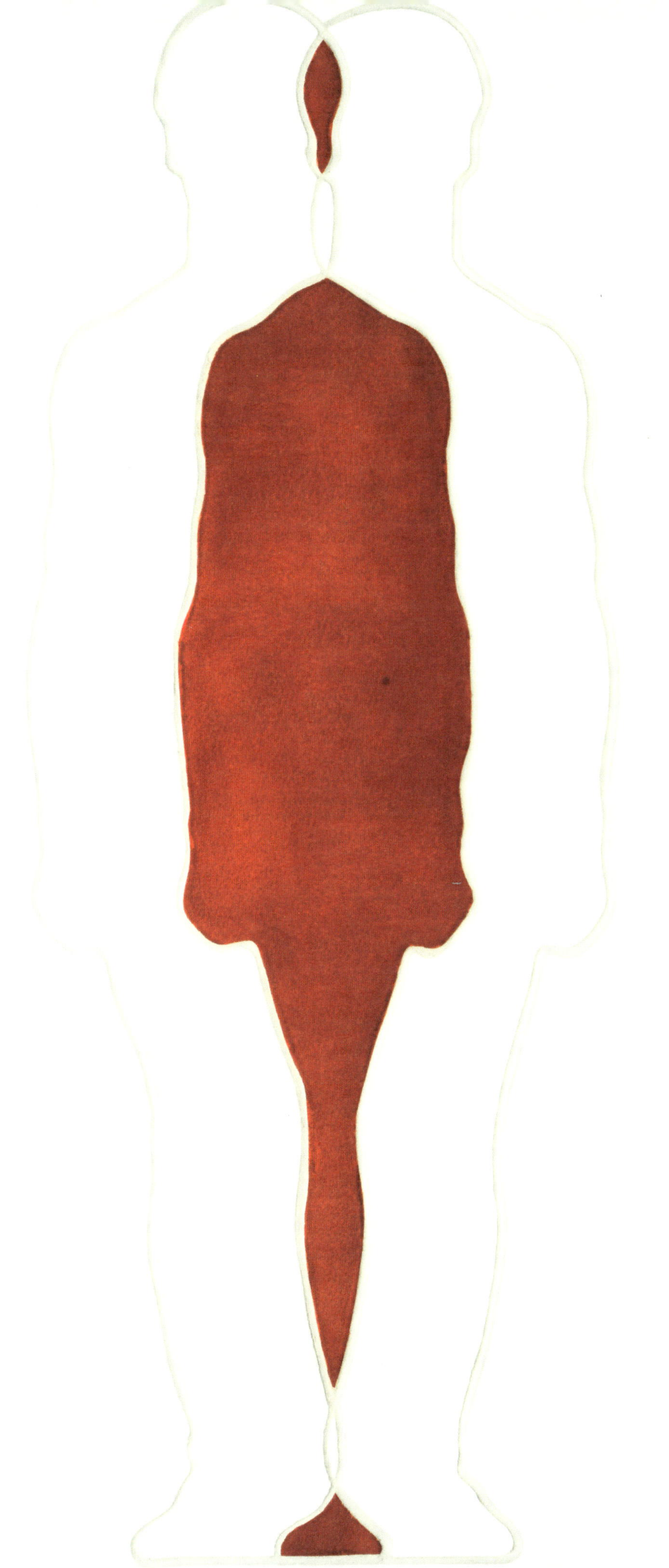

SHARE

Discover the ancestor.
Recognize our own mystery in him,
honoring him and letting go.

WHAT
CANNOT
BE
SEEN

Distinguish your own dreams from those you inherited.

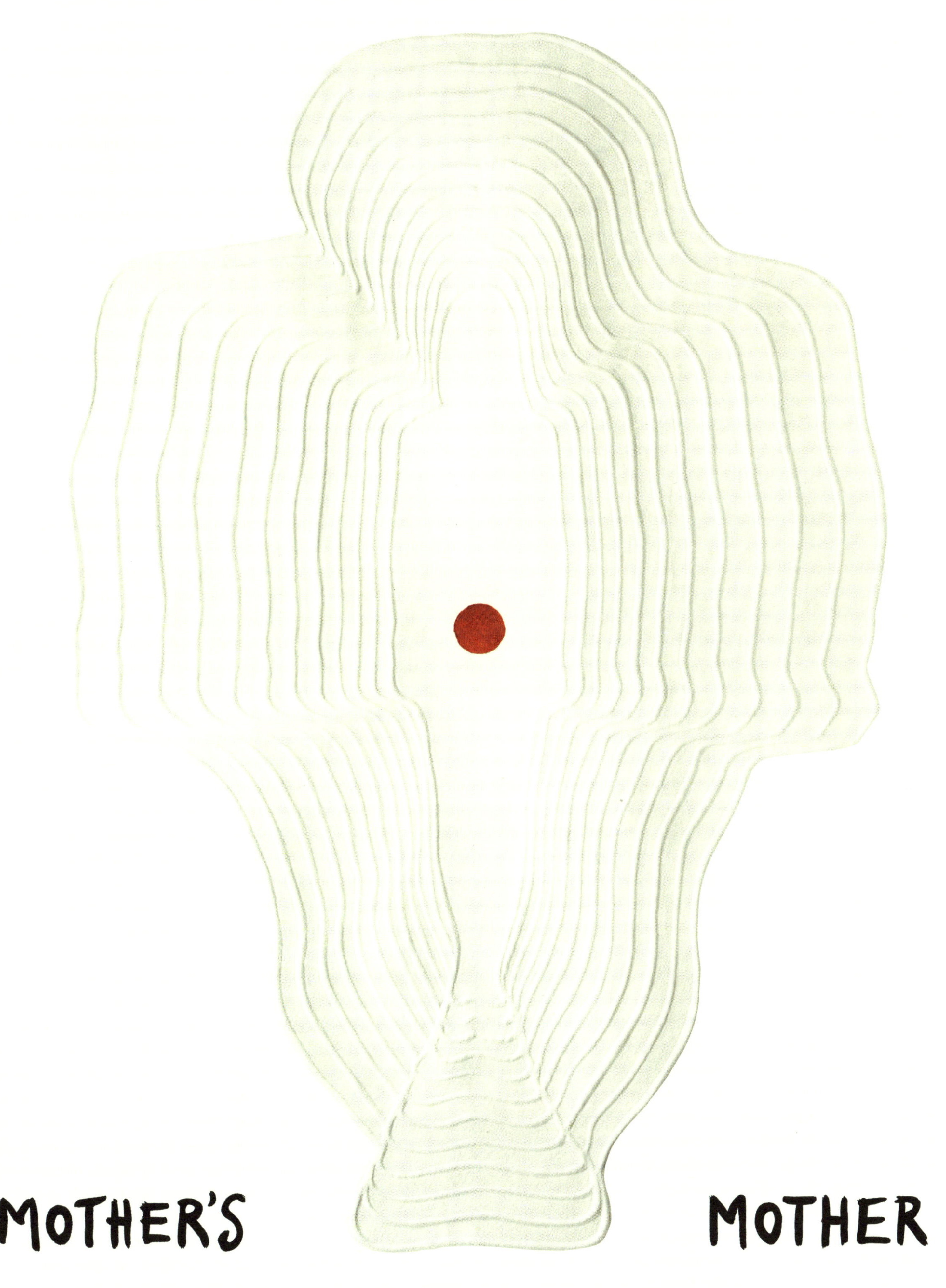
MOTHER'S
MOTHER

I am not me,
nor is my name my name.
I am parts of other beings.

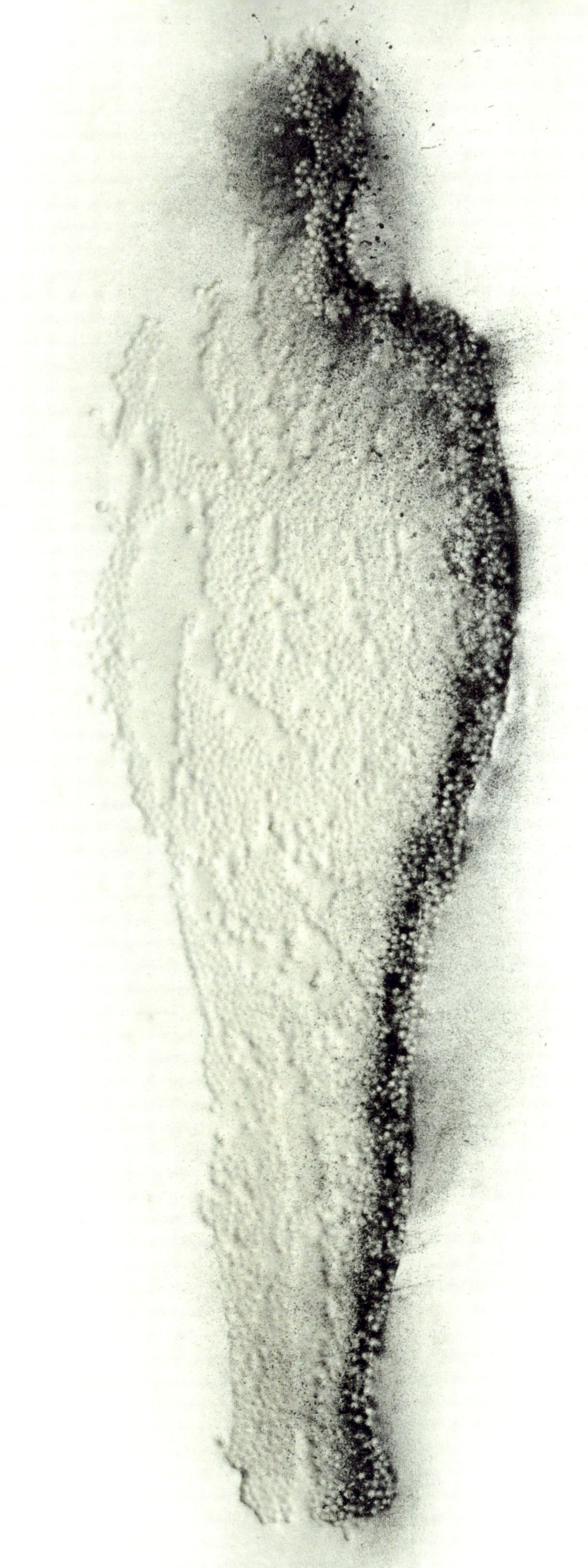

ME?

The stars, the world, me:
one and the same eternal matter.
This understood, loneliness ends.

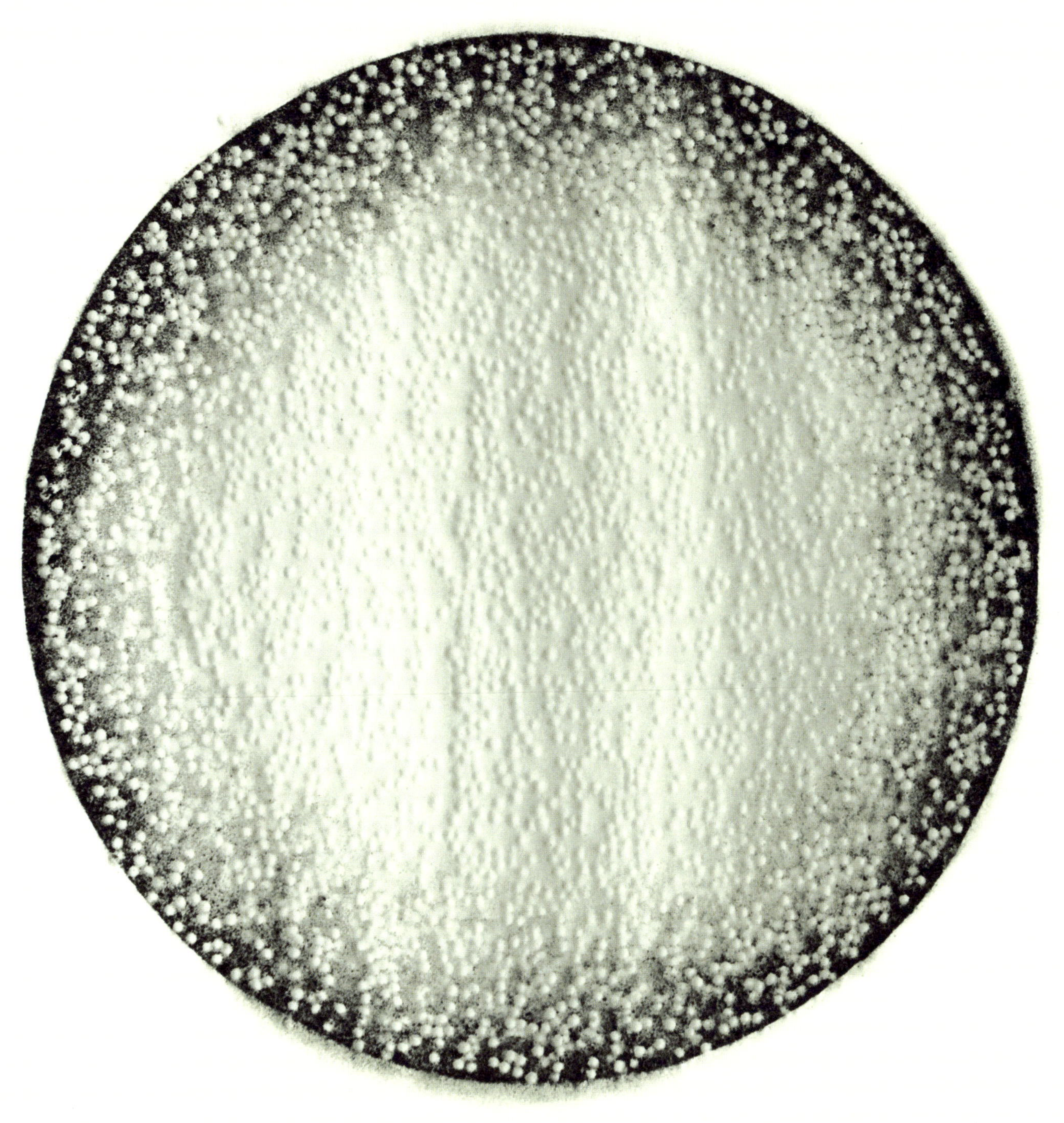

ETERNITY

Read the signs, which appear
when everything comes together effortlessly.

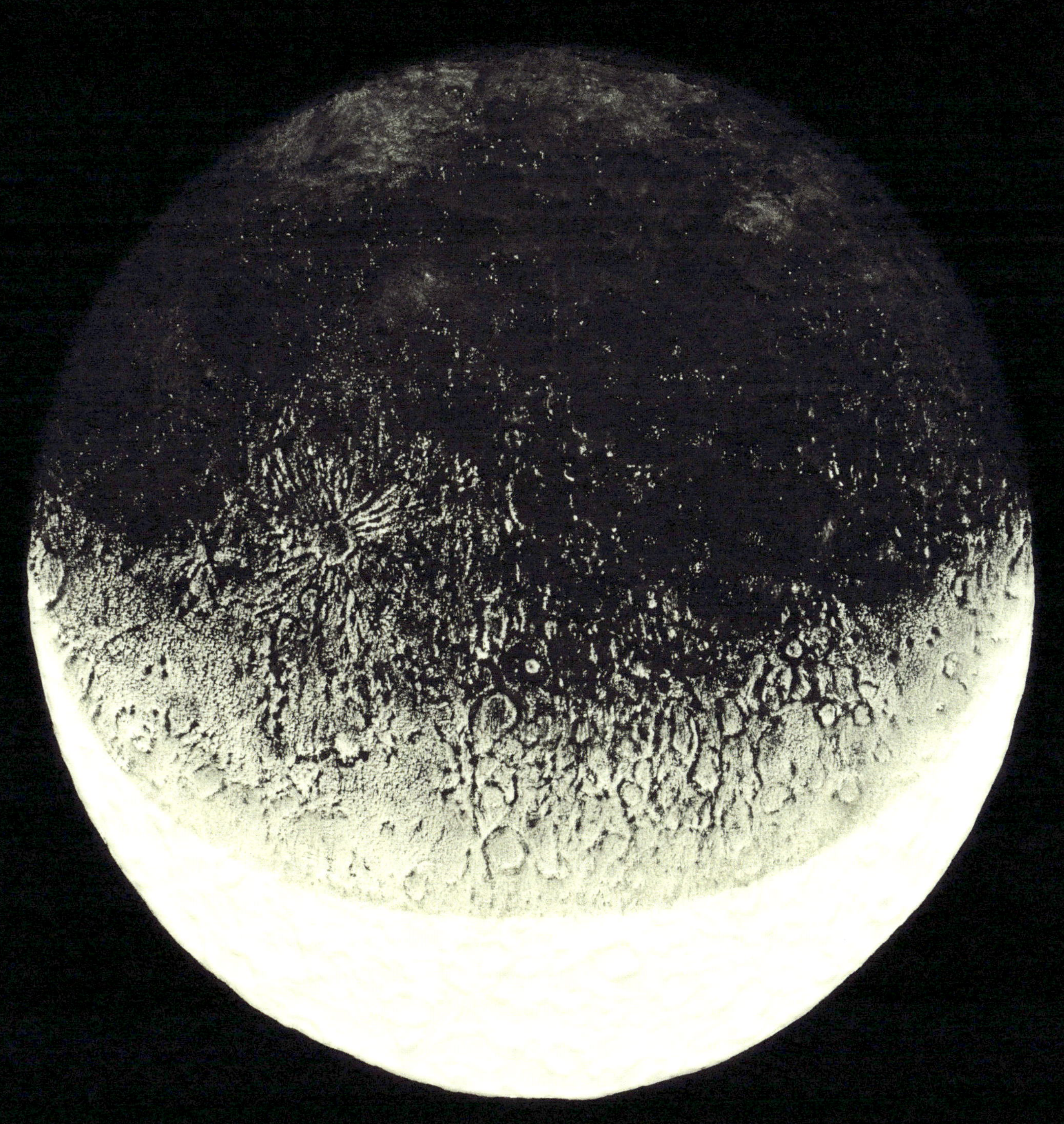

READ THE SIGNS

Seek Art
and discover Nature.

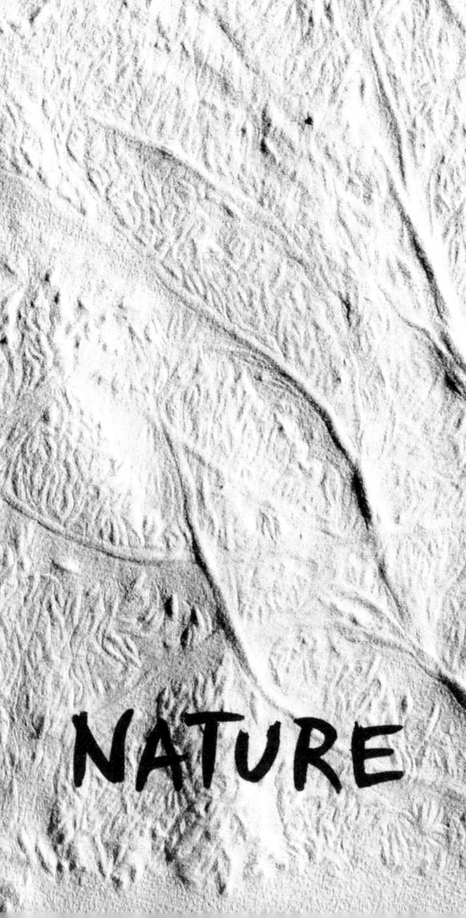
NATURE

You said this was the end
when it was in fact the beginning.

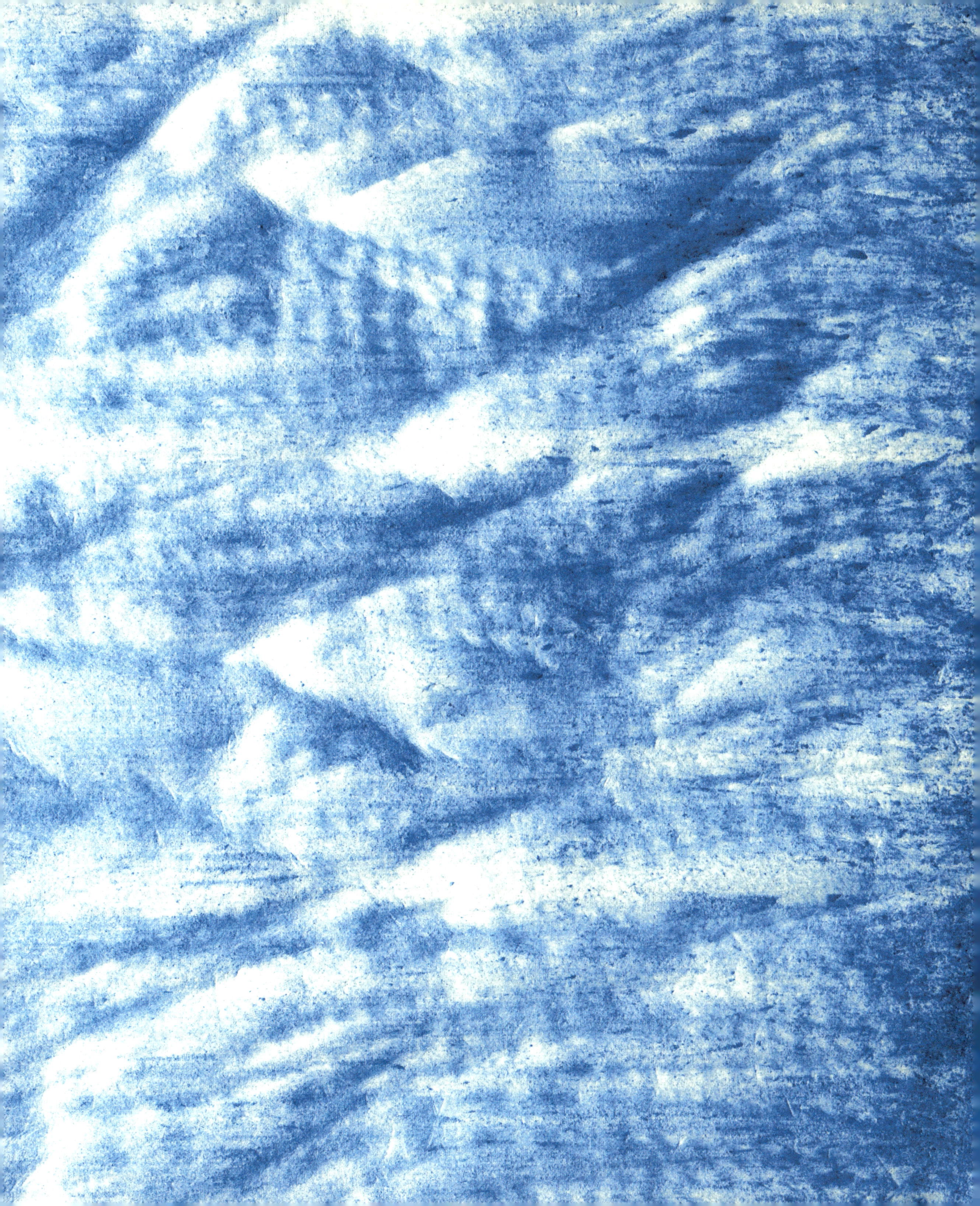

In turbulent times, when the old has still to disappear and the new is yet to arrive, Pepe Moll de Alba offers a thought-provoking and illuminating gaze where his artwork, delicate and wry, is coupled with a provocative poetic text. His work reveals the influences of light –its shadows– and the places he has lived; from the clarity that washes over his native Barcelona and the Canary Islands, where he spent his childhood marked by close contact with nature, to the gloom of Germany, where he was shaped as an artist, and the golden glow of Italy, where he matured as a painter. It is along these contrasts and tensions that he moves, as if he had somehow naturally blended the Tuscan Renaissance with the Bauhaus, creating an invisible bridge between them and his Atlantic and Mediterranean roots. Everything Pepe Moll de Alba creates is elegant and sensual, yet the root of his modernity is in his sincerity and courage. *Break Old Habits* manages to turn an autobiographical manifesto into a universal theme, inviting us to look deep within ourselves, making ours a story that is, today, more relevant than ever.

Vegueta Ediciones · **Ecolibri**

First Edition, May 2018
Originally published in Spanish as *Romper viejos hábitos*

Vegueta Ediciones
C/ Roger de Llúria 82, 08009 Barcelona, Spain
C/ General Bravo 26, 35002 Las Palmas de Gran Canaria, Spain
veguetaediciones.com

Photography: Eva Moll de Alba
Book Design: Pepe Moll de Alba

Printed and bound by Gràfiques Alzamora
ISBN: 978-84-17137-21-2
Spanish Legal Deposit: B 7075-2018

Printed in Spain

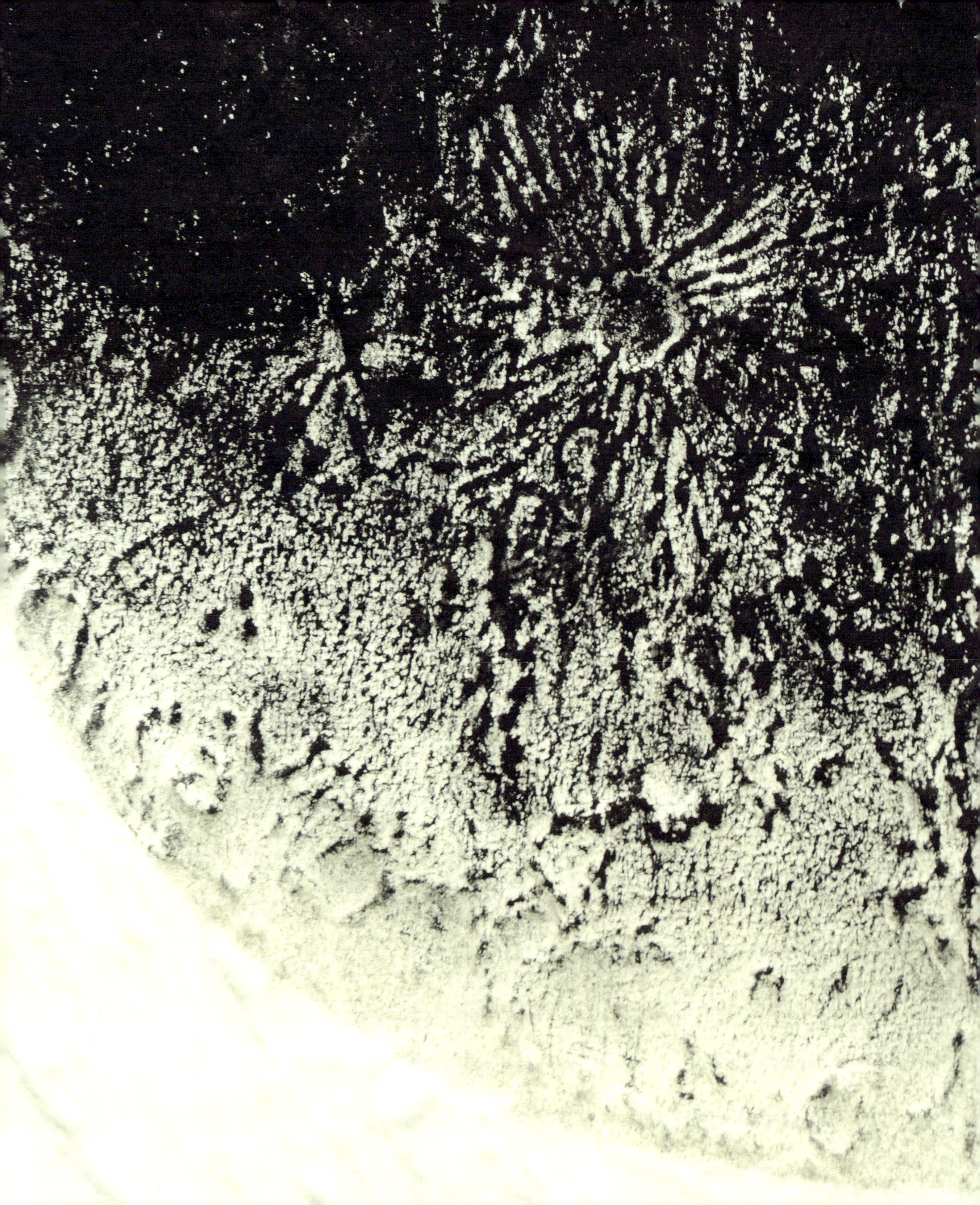